PUFFIN BOOKS

ANIMALS LIKE US

Animals Like Us is the perfect collection of animal poems for younger children. You will find every kind – from cats to caterpillars, sparrows to spiders, and horses to hedgehogs and they each take their turn in a wide-ranging collection which includes works by Allan Ahlberg, A. A. Milne, Kit Wright and Charles Causley. Fresh and accessible, with clear type and illustrations, *Animals Like Us* is bound to become a favourite with every young reader.

Tony Bradman was born and grew up in South London. After leaving university, he became a journalist and worked in the music press for several years. He then became Deputy Editor of *Parents* magazine, where he began to review children's books. He soon began writing his own, and published his first in 1984. In 1987 he gave up journalism to write for children full-time. He has written fiction, poetry and edited a number of anthologies. He still reviews for *Parents* and the *Daily Telegraph*, and lives in London with his wife and three children.

Other books by Tony Bradman

ADVENTURE ON SKULL ISLAND
CONTEST AT CUTLASS COVE
GERBIL CRAZY
MYSTERY AT MUSKET BAY
ONE NIL
PERIL AT THE PIRATE SCHOOL
SEARCH FOR THE SAUCY SALLY

Poetry

ALL TOGETHER NOW!
SMILE, PLEASE!

Collections chosen by Tony Bradman

HISSING STEAM AND WHISTLES BLOWING
THE BEST OF FRIENDS
THE MAD FAMILY
THE *PARENTS* BOOK OF BEDTIME STORIES
THAT SPELLS MAGIC
WHAT A WONDERFUL DAY!

Picture Book

THE SANDAL (with Philippe Dupasquier)

ANIMALS
LIKE US

chosen by
TONY BRADMAN

Illustrated by Madeleine Baker

Puffin Books

PUFFIN BOOKS

Published by the Penguin Group
Penguin Books Ltd, 27 Wrights Lane, London W8 5TZ, England
Penguin Books USA Inc., 375 Hudson Street, New York, New York 10014, USA
Penguin Books Australia Ltd, Ringwood, Victoria, Australia
Penguin Books Canada Ltd, 10 Alcorn Avenue, Toronto, Ontario, Canada M4V 3B2
Penguin Books (NZ) Ltd, 182–190 Wairau Road, Auckland 10, New Zealand

Penguin Books Ltd, Registered Offices: Harmondsworth, Middlesex, England

First published by Blackie and Son Ltd 1987
Published in Puffin Books 1989
3 5 7 9 10 8 6 4 2

This collection copyright © Tony Bradman, 1987
Illustrations copyright © Madeleine Baker, 1987
All rights reserved

Printed in England by Clays Ltd, St Ives plc

In these pages you will find
Animals of every kind,
Dogs and cats, alive and dead,
A lion that lives under a bed;
A goat that quacks, and what's that
        sound?
A hamster, going round and round . . .
Fish that swim and birds that fly,
And look! A hedgehog snuffling by.
Sheep and lambs, and there, in the road,
Something's moving — is it a toad?
There's a gerbil in some sand,
Reaching out to touch a hand,
For with the animals are people, too,
People just like me and you.
And animals like us, if you look,
All living and breathing, in this book!

Pet Shop

At our pet shop you can buy
Things that run and swim and fly,
But never once have I seen them sell
Anything as big as an el-
ephant or albatross,
Crocodile, bear, rhinoceros,
Nor ever a creature as small, alas,
As a kingfisher, or grass-
hopper, earwig, bumble-bee,
Minnow, mole or common flea.
O, I really think it is absurd
They don't keep a whale or a ladybird.

Leonard Clark

6

Our Hamster's Life

Our hamster's life:
there's not much
to it,
not much
to it.

He presses his pink nose
to the door of his cage
and decides for the fifty-six
millionth time
that he can't get
through it.

Our hamster's life;
there's not much
to it,
not much
to it.

It's about the most boring
life in the world,
if he only
knew it.

He sleeps and he drinks and he eats.
He eats and he drinks and he sleeps.
He slinks and he dreeps.
He eats.

This process
he repeats.

Our hamster's life:
there's not much
to it,
not much
to it.

You'd think it would drive him
bonkers,
going round and round on his wheel.
It's certainly driving me bonkers,

watching him
do it.

But he may be thinking:
'That boy's life,
there's not much
to it,

not much
to it:

watching a hamster go round
  on a wheel.
It's driving me bonkers if he only
  knew it

watching him
watching me
do it.'

> *Kit Wright*

Who rolled in the mud?

Who rolled in the mud
behind the garage door?
Who left footprints
across the kitchen floor?

I know a dog whose nose is cold
I know a dog whose nose is cold

Who chased raindrops
down the windows?
Who smudged the glass
with the end of his nose?

I know a dog with a cold in his nose
I know a dog with a cold in his nose

Who wants a bath
and a tuppenny ha'penny biscuit?
Who wants to bed down
in his fireside basket?

Me, said Ranzo
I'm the dog with a cold.

Mike Rosen

I Love Little Pussy

I love little pussy,
  Her coat is so warm,
And if I don't hurt her
  She'll do me no harm.
So I'll not pull her tail,
  Nor drive her away,
But pussy and I
  Very gently will play.
She shall sit by my side,
  And I'll give her some food.
And pussy will love me
  Because I am good.

Anon

11

Cat!

Cat!
Scat!
Atter her, atter her,
Sleeky flatterer,
Spitfire chatterer,
Scatter her, scatter her
   Off her mat!
   Wuff!
   Wuff!
   Treat her rough!
Git her, git her,
Whiskery spitter!
Catch her, catch her,
Green-eyed scratcher!
   Slathery
   Slithery
   Hisser,
   Don't miss her!
Run till you're dithery,
   Hithery
   Thithery!
   Pfitts! pfitts!
   How she spits!

Spitch! spatch!
Can't she scratch!
Scritching the bark
Of the sycamore tree,
She's reached her ark
And's hissing at me
Pfitts! pfitts!
Wuff! Wuff!
Scat,
Cat!
That's
That!

Eleanor Farjeon

13

Family Holiday

Eight months ago, on Christmas Day,
he was a present for the twins,
a toy to join in all their play.

They left by car, but how long since
he cannot tell, nor when they'll come
(if ever) back, to make amends.

The house is blind and deaf and dumb,
the curtains drawn, the windows shut,
the doors sealed tighter than a tomb.

Even the little garden hut
is padlocked. He barks feebly at
each slowing car or passing foot.

Stretched on the WELCOME on
    the mat
in the front porch, he feels the hunger
gnawing inside him like a rat.

Suffers, endures, but knows no anger.

Raymond Wilson

Cat in the Dark

Look at that!
Look at that!

But when you look
there's no cat.

Without a purr
just a flash of fur
and gone
like a ghost.

The most
you see
are two tiny
green traffic lights
staring at the
night.

John Agard

Our Cat

Our cat
was old and smelly

She liked
To lie before the telly

All curled
up around her grubby belly

I really loved that cat

She got
sick, and then much sicker

The vet
said she'd a dodgy ticker

He put
her down — no pain, and quicker

I really loved that cat

We brought
her home 'cause she was dead

Dad dug
a hole out by the shed

That night
I cried and cried and cried in bed

I really loved that cat

Now I've
no cat that's old and smelly

No cat
who lies before the telly

All curled
up around her grubby belly

I really loved that cat

Tony Bradman

A Little Cock Sparrow

A little cock sparrow sat on a
  green tree,
And he chirruped, he chirruped, so
  merry was he.
A naughty boy came with his wee
  bow and arrow,
Determined to shoot this little
  cock sparrow.
This little cock sparrow shall make
  me a stew,
And his giblets shall make me a
  little pie too.
Oh, no, said the sparrow, I won't
  make a stew,
So he flapped his wings, and away
  he flew.

Anon

18

I Held a Lamb

One day when I went visiting,
A little lamb was there,
I picked it up and held it tight,
It didn't seem to care.
Its wool was soft and felt so warm —
Like sunlight on the sand,
And when I gently put it down
It licked me on the hand.

Kim Worthington

The Donkey

I saw a donkey
One day old,
His head was too big
For his neck to hold;
His legs were shaky
And long and loose,
They rocked and staggered
And weren't much use.

He tried to gambol
And frisk a bit,
But he wasn't quite sure
Of the trick of it.
His queer little coat
Was soft and grey,
And he curled at his neck
In a lovely way.

He looked so little
And weak and slim,
I prayed the world
Might be good to him.

Anon

The Cow

The friendly cow all red and white,
  I love with all my heart:
She gives me cream with all her might,
  To eat with apple-tart.

She wanders lowing here and there,
  And yet she cannot stray,
All in the pleasant open air,
  The pleasant light of day;

And blown by all the winds that pass
And wet with all the showers,
She walks among the meadow grass
And eats the meadow flowers.

Robert Louis Stevenson

'Quack!' Said the Billy-Goat

'Quack!' said the billy-goat.
'Oink!' said the hen.
'Miaow!' said the little chick
Running in the pen.
'Hobble-gobble!' said the dog.
'Cluck!' said the sow.
'Tu-whit Tu-whoo!' the donkey said.
'Baa!' said the cow.
'Hee-haw!' the turkey cried.
The duck began to moo.
All at once the sheep went,
'Cock-a-doodle-doo!'
The owl coughed and cleared his throat
And he began to bleat.
'Bow-wow!' said the cock
Swimming in the leat.
'Cheep-cheep!' said the cat
As she began to fly.
'Farmer's been and laid an egg —
That's the reason why!'

Charles Causley

23

Flo the White Duck

All white and smooth is Flo
A-swimming;
Her lovely dress is plain . . .
No trimming.
A neat delight,
She fans to left and right
The silver rippled pond.
Behind her, safe and fond,
Her yellow ducklings bob and skim,
Yellow, fluffy, trim.

But all a-waddle and a-spraddle goes Flo
A-walking;
A clacking voice she has
For talking.
In slimy ooze
She plants enormous shoes
And squelches, squat and slow.

Behind her, in a row
Her ducklings dip and paddle
And try to spraddle.

Gwen Dunn

The Little Fish

I am a little fishy
I live down in the sea
I swim around
Without a sound

I like being me

Tony Bradman

I Had a Little Pony

I had a little pony,
  His name was Dapple-grey,
I lent him to a lady,
  To ride a mile away.

She whipped him, she lashed him,
  She drove him through the mire.
I wouldn't lend my pony now,
  For all the lady's hire.

  Anon

Natural History

The Dog will come when he is called,
  The Cat will walk away.
The Monkey's cheek is very bald,
  The Goat is fond of play.

The Parrot is a prate-apace,
Yet I know not what he says,
The noble Horse will win the race
 Or draw you in a chaise.

The Pig is not a feeder nice,
 The Squirrel loves a nut,
The Wolf would eat you in a trice,
 The Buzzard's eyes are shut.
The Lark sings high up in the air,
The Linnet in the tree;
The Swan he has a bosom fair,
 And who so proud as he?

Adelaide O'Keefe

Robin

If on a frosty morning
the robin redbreast calls
his waistcoat red and burning
like a beggar at your walls

throw breadcrumbs on the grass for him
when the ground is hard and still
for in his breast there is a flame
that winter cannot kill.

Iain Crichton Smith

Snake Glides

Snake glides
through grass
over
pebbles
forked tongue
working
never
speaking
but its
body
whispers
listen

Keith Bosley

Hedgehog

He ambles along like a walking pin
    cushion,
Stops and curls up like a chestnut burr.
He's not worried because he's so little.
Nobody is going to slap him around.

Chu Chen Po

Woodpecker

Carving
tap/tap
music

out of
tap/tap
tree trunk
keep me
busy
whole day
tap/tap
long

tap/tap
pecker
birdsong
tap/tap
pecker
birdsong

tree bark
is tap/tap
drumskin
fo me beak
I keep
tap/tap
rhythm
fo forest
heartbeat

tap/tap
chisel beak
long
tap/tap
honey leak
song
pecker/tap
tapper/peck
pecker
birdsong

John Agard

32

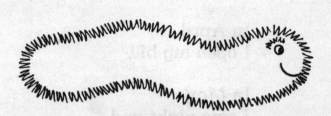

The Caterpillar

Brown and furry
Caterpillar in a hurry,
Take your walk
To the shady leaf, or stalk,
  Or what not,
Which may be the chosen spot.
  No toad spy you,
Hovering bird of prey pass by you;
Spin and die,
To live again as butterfly.

Christina Rossetti

The Cuckoo

Cuckoo, Cuckoo,
What do you do?

In April
I open my bill.

In May
I sing night and
day.

In June
I change my tune.

In July
Away I fly.

In August
Go I must.

Anon

When the Cows Come Home

When the cows come home the milk is
   coming;
Honey's made while the bees are
   humming;
Duck and drake on the rushy lake,
And the deer live safe in the breezy
   brake;
And timid, funny, pert little bunny
Winks his nose, and sits all sunny.

Christina Rossetti

The Nest

Don't move —
  don't touch —
don't speak —
  do you see
a blackbird's nest
  in the holly tree?

Look very carefully
  in between
last year's prickle
  and this year's green . . .

Timid and brown
  the mother bird
listens, and watches.
  Has she heard?

Whisper —
  whisper —
do you see

a blackbird's nest
in the holly tree?

Jean Kenward

Whisky Frisky

Whisky Frisky, hippity-hop
Up he goes to the treetop!

Whirly, twirly, round and round,
Down he scampers to the ground.

Furly, curly, what a tail!
Tall as a feather, broad as a sail!

Where's his supper? In the shell.
Snappity, crackity, out it fell.

Anon

The Gerbil

The gerbil stands up
Crouching like a kangaroo

Ready to hop;
To him the children he sees
Seem tall as trees;
His paws clutch
The teacher's hand
That stretches like a branch
Above the sand
Of the tiny desert
In his hutch.

Stanley Cook

Silverfish, Spiders and Flies

Small creatures see
That none of the space
In our classroom
Goes to waste

Silverfish keep warm
In cracks too small
Even for children's fingers
In the floor and against the wall.

And knitting their webs
The spiders fit
Onto ledges too narrow
For children to sit.

Flies stand on the ceiling
Or circle through the air
And even in PE
I never climbed up there.

Creatures that look
Like pips and seeds
Sow themselves in the places
No one else needs.

Stanley Cook

Upside Down

It's funny how beetles
and creatures like that
can walk upside down
as well as walk flat:

They crawl on a ceiling
and climb on a wall
without any practice
or trouble at all,

While I have been trying
for a year (maybe more)
and still I can't stand
with my head on the floor.

Aileen Fisher

41

The Fly

I live in a tower block
Where we're not allowed
To keep animals as pets
(Would they frighten the clouds?)

42

But I wanted a pet
And I've got one all right
It's a fly in a matchbox
(He lights up my nights)

Now maybe you think
That it's so bad of me —
But I really don't care
(He loves me, you see)

That fly in a matchbox
He's a buzzing good friend
He'll always stick by me
(Right up to . . . THE END)

Tony Bradman

Dog in the Playground

Dog in the playground
Suddenly there.
Smile on his face,
Tail in the air.

Dog in the playground
Bit of a fuss:
I know that dog —
Lives next to us!

Dog in the playground:
Oh, no he don't.
He'll come with me,
You see if he won't.

The word gets round;
The crowd gets bigger.
His name's Bob.
It ain't — it's Trigger.

They call him Archie!
They call him Frank!
Lives by the Fish Shop!

44

Lives up the Bank!
Who told you that?
Pipe down! Shut up!
I know that dog
Since he was a pup.

Dog in the playground:
We'll catch him, Miss.
Leave it to us.
Just watch this!

Dog in the playground
What a to-do!
Thirty-five children,
Caretaker too,
Chasing the dog,
Chasing each other.
He's our dog's brother!

We've cornered him now;
He can't get away.
Told you we'd catch him,
Robert and — Hey!
Don't open that door —
Oh, Glenis, you fool!

45

Look, Miss, what's happened:
Dog in the school.

Dog in the classroom,
Dog in the hall,
Dog in the toilets —
He's paying a call!
Forty-six children,
Caretaker too,
Headmaster, three teachers,
Hullabaloo!

Lost him! Can't find him!
He's vanished! And then:
Look, Miss, he's back
In the playground again.

Shouting and shoving —
I'll give you what for! —
Sixty-five children
Head for the door.

Dog in the playground,
Smile on his face,

46

Tail in the air,
Winning the race.

Dog in his element
Off at a jog,
Out of the gates:
Wish I was a dog.

Dog in the playground:
Couldn't he run?

Dog in the playground
      . . . Gone!

Allan Ahlberg

Odd

That's
odd
I must
say.

As I sat
on the
stump,
a piece of road
took
a lively
jump.

A small brown
clod
leaped
up
and away.

A piece of road!

Well, it *might*
have been
a tiny
toad.

Lillian Moore

Missing

Has anybody seen my mouse?

I opened his box for half a minute,
Just to make sure he was really in it,
And while I was looking, he jumped
   outside!
I tried to catch him, I tried, I tried . . .
I think he's somewhere about the house.
Has *anyone* seen my mouse?

Uncle John, have you seen my mouse?

Just a small sort of mouse, a dear little
   brown one,
He came from the country, he wasn't a
   town one,
So he'll feel all lonely in a London street;
Why, what could he possibly find to
   eat?

He must be somewhere. I'll ask
   Aunt Rose:
Have *you* seen a mouse with a
   woffelly nose?
Oh, somewhere about —
He's just got out . . .

Hasn't *anybody* seen my mouse?

A. A. Milne

My Brother Bert

Pets are the Hobby of my Brother Bert.
He used to go to school with a Mouse in
   his shirt.

His Hobby it grew, as some hobbies will,
And grew and Grew and GREW until —

Oh don't breathe a word, pretend you
   haven't heard.
A simply appalling thing has occurred —

The very thought makes me iller
   and iller:
Bert's brought home a gigantic Gorilla!

52

If you think that's really not such
  a scare,
What if it quarrels with his
  Grizzly Bear?

You still think you could keep your head?
What if the Lion from under the bed

And the four Ostriches that deposit
Their football eggs in his bedroom
  closet

And the Aardvark out of his bottom
  drawer
All danced out and joined in the Roar?

What if the Pangolins were to caper
Out of their nests behind the wallpaper?

With the fifty sorts of Bats
That hang on his hatstand like old hats,

And out of a shoebox the excitable
  Platypus
Along with the Ocelot
  or Jungle-Cattypus?

The Wombat, the Dingo, the Gecko, the
  Grampus —
How they would shake the house with
  their Rumpus!

Not to forget the Bandicoot
Who would certainly peer from his
  battered old boot.

Why it could be a dreadful day,
And what Oh what would the
  neighbours say!

Ted Hughes

The Goat

There was a man, now please take note,
There was a man, who had a goat,
He loved that goat, indeed he did,
He loved that goat, just like a kid.

One day that goat felt frisk and fine,
Ate three red shirts from off the line.
The man he grabbed him by the back,
And tied him to a railroad track.

But when the train hove into sight,
That goat grew pale and green
    with fright.
He heaved a sigh, as if in pain,
Coughed up those shirts and flagged
    the train.

Anon

White Horses

Count the white horses you meet on
    the way,
Count the white horses, child, day
    after day,
Keep a wish ready for wishing — if you
Wish on the ninth horse, your wish will
    come true.

I saw a white horse at the end of
    the lane,
I saw a white horse canter down by
    the shore,
I saw a white horse that was drawing
    a wain,
And one drinking out of a trough:
    that made four.

I saw a white horse gallop over the
    down,
I saw a white horse looking over a gate,
I saw a white horse on the way into
    town,

And one on the way coming back: that
  made eight.

But oh for the ninth one: where *he*
  tossed his mane,
And cantered and galloped and
  whinnied and swished
His silky white tail, I went looking
  in vain,
And the wish I had ready could never
  be wished.

Count the white horses you meet on
  the way,
Count the white horses, child, day
    after day,
Keep a wish ready for wishing — if you
Wish on the ninth horse, your wish will
    come true.

  Eleanor Farjeon

Sheep in Winter

The sheep get up and make their many
    tracks
And bear a load of snow upon their
    backs,
And gnaw the frozen turnip to the
    ground
With sharp, quick bite, and then go
    noising round
The boy that pecks the turnips all
    the day
And knocks his hands to keep the cold
    away
And laps his legs in straw to keep
    them warm
And hides behind the hedges from
    the storm.
The sheep, as tame as dogs, go where
    he goes
And try to shake their fleeces from the
    snows,

Then leave their frozen meal and
　　wander round
The stubble stack that stands beside
　　the ground,
And lie all night and face the drizzling
　　storm
And shun the hovel where they might
　　be warm.

John Clare

To Market, To Market

To market, to market,
To buy a fat pig . . .
Home again, home again,
Jiggety jig!

To market, to market,
To buy a fat hog . . .
Home again, home again,
Jiggety jog!

Anon

Index of First Lines

Acknowledgements

The author and the Publishers would like to thank the following for their kind permission to use copyright material in this anthology:

The Bodley Head for 'Cat in the Dark' by John Agard from *I Din Do Nuttin;* John Agard for 'Woodpecker' by John Agard; Penguin Books for 'Dog in the Playground' from *Please Mrs Butler* by Allan Ahlberg (Kestrel Books 1983) copyright © Allan Ahlberg; Keith Bosley for 'Snake Glides' from *And I Dance* by Keith Bosley; David Higham Assocs Ltd for ' "Quack!" Said the Billy Goat' from *Figgie Hobbin* by Charles Causley; The Estate of Leonard Clark for 'Pet Shop' by Leonard Clark; Iain Crichton Smith for 'Robin'; Stanley Cook for 'The Gerbil' and 'Silverfish, Spiders and Flies' from *Come Along* by Stanley Cook; Gwen Dunn for 'Flo the White Duck'; David Higham Assocs Ltd for 'Cat!' and 'White Horses' from *Silver Sand and Snow* by Eleanor Farjeon; Aileen Fisher for 'Upside Down' from *Up the Windy Hill;* Faber and Faber for 'My Brother Bert' from *Meet My Folks* by Ted Hughes; Jean Kenward for 'The Nest' from *Here We Go;* Methuen Children's Books and McClelland & Stewart, Toronto, for 'Missing' from *When We Were Very Young* by A A Milne; Lillian Moore and Atheneum Publishers for 'Odd' by Lillian Moore from *Little Raccoon and Poems from the Woods;* New Directions Publishing Corporation and Kenneth Rexroth for 'Hedgehog' from *One Hundred Poems from the Chinese*, copyright © Kenneth Rexroth 1971; André Deutsch and Michael Rosen for 'Who Rolled in the Mud' from *Mind Your Own Business* by Michael Rosen; Raymond Wilson for 'Family Holiday'; Collins Publishers for 'Our Hamster's Life' from *Rabbiting On* by Kit Wright.

Every attempt has been made to trace the copyright holders and the Publishers apologize if any inadvertent omission has been made.